SHUPTON'S FANCY

SHUPTON'S FANCY

A TALE
OF THE FLY-FISHING
OBSESSION

PAUL SCHULLERY

STACKPOLE
BOOKS

Copyright © 1996 by Paul Schullery
Published by
STACKPOLE BOOKS
5067 Ritter Road
Mechanicsburg, PA 17055

All inquiries should be addressed to:

Stackpole Books
5067 Ritter Road
Mechanicsburg, PA 17055
Printed in the United States of America
10 9 8 7 6 5 4 3 2 1
First edition

This is a work of fiction. Any resemblance between characters
or places in this book and any actual person living or dead or places past
or present is purely coincidental. An obvious exception to this are the
numerous fishing writers mentioned, who are known public figures.

Library of Congress Cataloging-in-Publication Data
Schullery, Paul.
    Shupton's fancy: a tale of the fly-fishing obsession/Paul Schullery. —1st ed.
      -p.   cm.
    ISBN 0-8117-1534-5
    1. Americans—Travel—England—Fiction. 2. Fly fishing—England—Fiction.
3. Fly tying—England—Fiction. I. Title.
PS3569. c5366S58   1996
813.54—dc20
                                    96-769
                                    CIP

FOR DAVID LEDLIE

The Dorset Inn
Friday, June 10

Dear Al,

What was it Halford said about the train ride from London to the Itchen—how you step out "amongst all the long-desired things?" Well, I'm among them at last, with the Dorset whispering its way past my window. After a more harrowing than usual flight, and the obligatory Heathrow Transdimensional Crisis (reeling out of the lot on the wrong side of the road, reflexively trying to reach out of the right-hand window of one of those wretched dinky rentals to grab some ancestral gearshift . . .), and two days in Londontown with my publisher's British toadies, my train was a balm and a blessing, and now I'm in for a weekend here at the inn. I couldn't see it well in the dark, but Stan says the water is in fine shape for a good rise in the morning.

All is the same. I recognize every lump in the mattress. Dot and Stan are fine, fat as ever and just as able in the kitchen (how they survived their culture's crippling effects on good cuisine I can't imagine), and (I know

you're waiting to hear) Megan eases toward her thirties with sublime grace. My God, what is on the minds of the local swains, that they haven't lined up for a try at her? If I were even ten years younger (and even fifty pounds lighter, though any more that's hardly enough to show), I'd fill out an application myself. My kingdom for some prolonged eye contact.

I'm settled in the library, speaking of long-desired things, with an appropriate stout, a good pipe, and no goals until morning, and I find that I now have the leisure to censure you more comprehensively for not coming along. Your excuse of only six hours' notice is all too feeble for me, Al; used to be you'd fish anywhere at a moment's notice.

So here's what you didn't let me explain on the phone. My agent finally talked a satisfactorily fat publisher (Collins-Marstowe, if it means anything to you) into the "Great Dinners of History" (or some similar bilge of a title, "history's greatest porkouts," or whatever) cookbook—my long and brilliant sales record, my erudition in all things culinary, blah blah blah. I'm to write the coffee-table cookbook to end all such extravaganzas, a

veritable hotel of a book, where you can check in and get to know the staff. With a regal advance on the way, I saw no reason to waste a chance at the season over here, so I'm going to hit the stream between stints at the Bodleian and the British Museum. Even London food can't dull my appetite for a good manuscript binge; I do love a library.

Your role, of course, is to react jealously to my accounts of piscatorial triumph and the excesses of Dot's table. I will be merciless.

Yours,

F. Martin

London
The Hampson
Monday, June 13

Al,

My taunts backfired; it rained like the proverbial cow the entire weekend, and I never even made a cast.

Arrived here and waddled out of the train feeling like a beached whale from Dot's magnificent dinners. She gets her flour from some other planet; I can sense a gravitational differential in the loaves, as if they were meant to rest on sturdier tables somewhere far, far away.

I know you don't share my passion for a good literature search, so I'll spare you the high points of my week here, except to rejoice briefly that they've finally accessioned a whole batch of medieval manuscript material that has been languishing in some bibliographical dungeon since "right after the war" (When I asked him "which war?" the heron of a head librarian just drew a bead on me down his nose, sniffed, and continued his admonishments about the criminality of ball-point pens).

Maybe by reading this old stuff I'll finally discover where Limey cooking went wrong; it surely had to have been several centuries ago, in order to have declined this far.

Martin

London
Thursday, June 16

A.,

I'm off to the river again tonight, with better prospects for some sunshine and shadow. At dawn I'm going straight to the Dame's bend for a look. If she's rising, I'll dedicate my broken tippet to you.

Back to my pipe.

M.

London
Monday, June 20

A.,

Rain again, like sheets the whole weekend. No fishing, no Dame, no rise. But Megan almost smiled at something silly I said during dinner (she was serving again—I don't remember a thing on the plate). I'd swear

in court I saw her lip get ready to turn up, just a bit, like someone who hadn't really almost smiled, but had thought about the idea of almost smiling and subconsciously sent a few electrons down that way, just to test out the circuits.

M.

London
Wednesday, June 22

Al,

Finally got into the new manuscripts today. Slow going, an endless number of almost illegible little pieces of thick, cardboardy stuff, each one sandwiched in its own special acid-free folder, served up one at a time by the sour-faced little librarian I think of as the Book Nazi. Doesn't matter if the damn paper only has four words on it; I have to fill out a form, turn it over to the BN, and wait while she knuckles off into the catacombs for a while (probably has a sailor back there) and then carries it out to my little table like she's serving up Charlemagne's

testicles on a croissant, where I feel obliged to pretend gratitude (each time, of course) and that such a sacred thing will require great amounts of my time. I pick it up with my little cotton gloves (the fingers are never as long as mine), reread the four words about twenty times, just so the interval is tasteful, then return it to its folder and give it back with another request form, and the BN takes the form from me like she's never seen me before.

I don't really need to do all this. I could pirate a thousand sufficiently picturesque recipes from all the books that have totally exhausted my subject (but not the market) over the past 150 years. But I love being in here, touching such old, real, rare things. Most of them are stupendously dull—"Pyke out the best connes and do hem in a pot of erthe, do therto whyte grece, that he stewe therinne, and lye hem up with hony clarified and with rawe yolkes and with a lytell almaund mylke; and do therinne powdour fort and safroun, and loke that it be yleesshed." Get that? It's more cogent than most (in fact, I'm so used to it that this one sounds familiar, even tasty). These old cooks operated without everything today's prissy food snoots take for granted, all the little comfort-

ing amenities like baking temperatures and times, proportions, and measurements. This stuff reminds me of my Aunt Polly, who always responded to requests for her recipes with, "Oh, you know, a mouthful of this, a mouthful of that."

But for all that, I'm the first person, the first even vaguely scholar-like person, to see this stuff since its creation half a millennium ago. That has a lot of value to me. But I can see you're bored already, so I'll let it go. There's hope for clearer weather this weekend.

Marty

The Dorset
Saturday night, June 25

Al,

It was the Dame, and for an instant this morning she was mine. She rose for me, Al, and I left my tiniest BWO no-hackle in her hinge—Just for a gasp, I saw the leader tighten and zing free of the surface film and run straight to the back of her jaw; then the tippet parted and the line

noodled back toward me. Shit, of course, but Glory Be at the same time! Not a genuine BWO in sight, but something told me it would strike her fancy.

If memory serves, that's seven hookups for me, five for you. And, of course, twelve escapes for the Dame. Figuring in time invested, my per-hour hookup rate is now .2, and yours is .25, so I'm gaining on you.

Stan made all the appropriately obsequious and congratulatory noises upon my return. Bless him, I think his enthusiasm is genuine, though I can't imagine why after all these years of sucking up to nearsighted barristers and fat foreigners. Megan, of course, said not a word. But I think she gave me more of that sublime whiskey cake than usual, though it may have been my imagination. It certainly gave me "dreams in Technicolor," as my Aunt Verna used to say. I wonder if that's why walruses took to the water—they just got too fat to sleep on the ground without nightmares.

After my triumph with the Dame, knowing I couldn't repeat it in the same weekend, I may return to town tomorrow. I've noticed something interesting in the manuscripts and I'm anxious to get an early start Monday so I can follow it.

Tight reels, screaming lines, and all of that,
Martin

London
Friday, July 1

Al,

I'm definitely onto something here. I can't quite tell you how I know, but I feel like I've stumbled onto some oddly important little thing that won't let go of my attention.

Last Friday, the umpteenth little fragment of manuscript wasn't quite so little. It was a collection of recipes (it's felonious to call such incomplete things recipes, but you don't care), and faintly marked at the bottom of the last "page" (I'm sure you don't want a digression on folios and such) were what I take to be initials—WW.

Now any medieval British literature geek would right

off recognize William Worcester (1415–1482) as the most likely signatory. This was kind of exciting, to actually recognize someone, especially someone like WW, who was my kind of antiquary; loved to save recipes and remedies, all that sort of thing. I even shared my discovery with the heron, who, in a blaze of untoward interest, sighted me in *across* the bridge of his nose with his left eye while raising his right eyebrow (I later tried to do this, in private of course, and couldn't). I had no real use for the information, but it was almost sexually satisfying that no one among the library's catalogers had identified this little tidbit, while I had.

That happened last week, as I say. Then, just as I was about to give up for the day yesterday, I came upon another signed WW manuscript. This one I took the time to check against a known sample of his writing (it matched, mostly), and it kept me awake all night. It also has entirely sidetracked me from "Great Hog Troughs of the Ancients." Most of it was as dull as the rest have been. It was a recipe for some kind of ghastly fish chowder (at least that's as close to a generic description as I can come for something so execrably described). But at the end was this little note, in the same hand but a little sep-

arate from the rest, like it was an afterthought added the next day. It was almost like an advertisement, Al, the only time so far I've seen one of these old birds tell you where to go to get your raw materials.

Just to make sure you appreciate it, I'm going to modernize it, to spare you the primitive spelling. It ran like this, "And the best fish for this pottage [odd use of this word in this context, but you don't care] is to be got from one A. Shptn, who takes his fish ["fysch," if you were wondering] on every throw."

What is this, Al? Is it mere promotional hype? This guy "Shptn" is a good bet for fresh fish, in fact he's your best bet because he never fails to catch fish, so his fish are always fresher? Is it an early old-boy system—I'll tell lies about you if you tell them about me? Or was this guy really good? And what the hell did he "throw?" Bait? Lures? Nets? Flies? *Flies?*

Now you may think this a minor thing to get so worked up about, but I don't suppose you read enough to know better. If you were to read something besides those trendy "White Man's Gravity Sports" magazines, you might understand. Here's what I remembered, as I sat staring at that sentence.

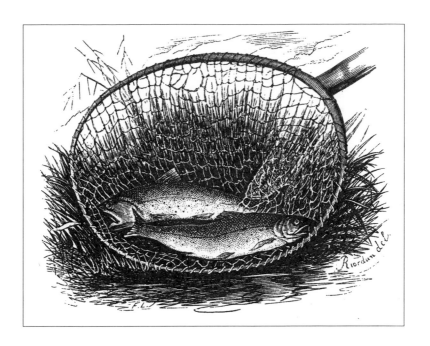

Back about 1980 or '81, a Belgian linguist named Braekman published an absolutely charming little book on the *Treatyse*. Among other things, he reported on some previously unidentified manuscripts that are contemporary with, or predate, that book. Now Braekman apparently wasn't all that solid in some of his homework—the Canadian medievalist, Hoffmann, said something about him being "cavalier" in his editorializing. But Braekman had found his way to some amazing new stuff—fly-tying advice, that sort of thing—that predates the 1496 publication of the *Treatyse,* which, of course, generations of fishermen (who are hopeless ancestor worshipers) have slobbered over as the fly fisherman's Old Testament.

For all Braekman's problems, his findings are great fun. What some of us found most intriguing was his mention of an actual fifteenth-century fisherman. It seemed he found the name of a guy, Anthony Shupton, with some of this fishing manuscript stuff, and figured the chap was a local sport from 500 years ago. Imagine.

Well, let's see, it was about '84 or '85, during my fling with the California crowd, I was over here with the usual abundant wherewithal, so I went to the British Library and tracked the Shupton thing down for myself. Sure

enough, the name was real (though the Library spelled it Sheepton in their catalog). Besides that, it seemed that the whole thing had been gathered by William Worcester! But as I looked it over, I thought Braekman was kind of reaching to attribute the fishing stuff to Shupton (Hoffmann was right about his carelessness), whose name only appeared later in the manuscript, not even on the same pages as the fishing stuff. That made me doubt that we could count on Shupton as even being a fisherman. It all sounded a little thin, but who could forget the name after the initial kick of such an introduction? Not me.

So it pretty much jumped out at me this time, and it's still got my attention. As I say, I have this feeling about it. Well, it's more than a feeling. It's like when I obsessed about tarpon—remember? It's taken hold of me; I even forgot lunch. That hasn't happened since that morning off No Name Key.

Uplifting as this is, I must go. The train approaches, and I need a weekend just to let this all settle. Maybe Megan will distract me, for all the good it will do us from across the room.

Marty

Sunday, July 15, or 16, or something like that

Al,

Sorry to lose touch, but you'll understand. Well, no you won't, but you'll listen, and anyway, I need to talk some of this out. Let's see, where did I leave this—I should have backed up the file on this damn notebook. I guess I wrote last while waiting for the train to the river.

Well, I didn't go. Or, I went, but I just came right back. I figured I couldn't sit still or fish through a whole weekend, and that maybe somewhere in London I'd find something open, a library or a records center or something, that would let me keep working and thinking about Shupton, so I waited at the station (sent Stan home—he was there right on time to pick me up) until a return train came along, and caught it back to town.

I'm on the great hunt of my life, Al, and I'm on a hot trail. I can't tell you too much. More accurate, I *shouldn't* tell you too much. If this leads where I think it might, I don't want anybody but me to be responsible for what I find. But I'll give you a general outline of what I'm up to. I'm still in London, but I've been out of town a couple times, here and there.

I'm determined to track down this Shupton guy.
Having no leads at all on him, though, I started with
William Worcester, which led me to certain records col-
lections, which led me to certain villages, and so on,
chasing around in church records, county records,
archives, estate lists, anything that seemed like a warm
scent. Most of it was a waste of time, but really, England
500 years ago wasn't all that crowded a place, and if
someone had some substance, they might get their name
written down a few times, maybe even on a tombstone or
a deed. Then all that had to happen was that all the sub-
sequent Kings and Queens and City Fathers didn't find
some stupid reason to burn the church or move the
county seat or pave the graveyard, and there I'd have it.

Well, I don't have it yet, Al, but I think I'm getting
close. I know, I know, right now you're muttering,
"Don't have *what,* fat boy?" Hold on, and I'll get there. In
a kind of run-down basement archives, in a more than
run-down county building, in a less than desirable piece
of real estate not all that far from here, I was looking
through some stuff on microfilm (it was the *original*
microfilm reader, Al, maybe even a prototype—looked
sort of like a mutant composter, and I'd swear it was
steam driven). The connection of this place to WW was

tenuous, but it seemed he had some pals or distant rela-tives in the area, but the WW biography has some holes in it, so it was hard to tell, but, as I said before, the scent seemed warm, so there I was, just back from a bilious lunch at the local sty, and grinding through the microfilm between eructations. It wasn't looking good.

Then I come upon an estate list, you know, one of those tallies of some dead guy's property, and I recognize the name—he's an occasional correspondent of WW! So I run through the list, my fingertip going up and down the screen on each sheet, and all at once I have it—the debts. Seems things were, uh, financially slow in 1457, and my subject crossed the river without settling up. Owed half the county, including the transaction I was looking for—one "Aty. Shoptn," owed for two "fschng rds [why did these people hate vowels so much?] and divers dobs." Translation, Shupton sold him some fish-ing rods and a bunch of flies (they called them dobs, or dubs, as in "dubbing," sometimes). So he was a fly tier. So it could have been a *fly* that allowed him to catch fish at will!

That was good enough, but just a little way down the same list, here was my man Shupton again ("A. Shptn"

this time), this time taking a loss on what I think was some kind of building or carpentry work. I not only had a fisherman, I had a dealer in fishing tackle, and I had a tradesman. And that's what I'm working on now.

I guess I ought to check in with Stan—they were expecting me, what, two or three weeks ago. I can't go back there now, Al. It's looking too good.

Martin

July 30, but I don't know what day of the week, Tuesday, I think

Al,

I can't get the fly out of my mind now. If he really had a fly that always worked, or even worked extraordinarily well, what would it be?

I know one thing for sure, it had to be a wet fly. Whatever Cameron and Heddon and Ledlie and the rest of those self-important revisionist giant-killers may have proved about the antiquity of floating flies, it has always been obvious to me that most fish are taken below the

surface, and most flies have been fished below the surface. Shupton was apparently in this for a living, and he wasn't likely to dink around with something as time-wasting as a fly that must float.

I also figure it couldn't be a precise imitation—we have too many of those today, and some of them work pretty well but none of them are miraculous, and I'm assuming (I guess) that this fly was pretty much never-fail, like my mother's pie crust.

See, too many modern fishermen naively assume that those guys centuries ago were somehow stupid just because they didn't have nylon and graphite; actually, they were probably sharper and more observant than we are. After all, they *lived* on the water, and illiterate isn't the same as unperceptive. But, giving them that much, one of the few things I think we probably *can* (God, I love italics—maybe I was supposed to grow up to be Schwiebert) do today is make a much more accurate imitation than they could, right down to the operculate gill thingies, and all that kind of microscope stuff that was beyond the technology or knowledge of the fifteenth century.

So, if it wasn't a precise imitation, it must have been what the Victorians referred to as a "fancy" pattern. The designation didn't necessarily mean frilly or gaudy, though that's what they did to the fancy fly eventually, with all their jungle cocks and silver monkeys and married wings and overdressing; it just meant that the fly's intentions and design were not aimed at anything in particular, but at a pleasing kind of hopefulness of appearance that might work for whatever reason.

So I'm now calling it Shupton's Fancy, and I figure it's going to be just a little surprising. I kind of expect it to be mostly very ordinary, but with one or two features that really raise the eyebrow at first glance.

But what are they? What haven't we tried, the millions of us over the last 500 years, furiously tying away generation after generation, adding every possible fiber and hair and gimcrack? What could Shupton have done, on his end of this long, long episode of experimentation, that a whole lot of other people wouldn't stumble on later? Was it some strange material? Did he give it some action we haven't thought of? So many questions!

And most of all, would he tell anyone? And even more most of all, would he tell me? Would he be able to

resist leaving a message for someone, anyone, letting them in on this wondrous gift he'd found?

Of course if I didn't think so, I wouldn't be here. I'm betting I understand human nature; I'm betting that no one could keep that secret.

I know what you're thinking, Al. You're thinking I've lost it. I don't even know if the story was true in the first place. Maybe WW was just promoting a friend—I don't even know if this Shupton guy was really able to catch a fish on every cast, much less if he did it with flies. Objectively, I know you could be right. After all, in another one of his texts, WW did describe a mysterious bait ointment that was shown him by "a cunning angler." Maybe, you would say, that was Shupton. Maybe, you would object if you were here, this Shupton, if he was that good a fisherman, just had some kind of goop he put on his bait that attracted lots of fish. Well, you go ahead and think that if you want, but you're not here. I know there's more to it than that; I can just feel it. There's a fly in this, and it's important.

Stay tuned. Maybe I can find out. I hope so. I haven't slept two hours a night for a month, and if I have to eat very many more meals of this British dog poop, I'll bust.

Marty

Early August, more or less

Al,

I foolishly lost the trail there for a while. Spent almost a week looking around that grubby little thatch-patch where I found the estates list, assuming that if Shupton sold the guy stuff, and built him something, he must have lived there somewhere *near* the guy. Finally I went back to the archives, did some more digging, and found out that the guy had lived for several years about fifty miles away, in a slightly more prosperous village. So I went there, thinking that maybe Shupton had lived in that town too, and hit a sort of pay dirt almost immediately.

It was Shupton's town, all right, and the church and the courthouse and the records were in much better shape, and I found several pieces of paper with his name on them. Seems he was more than a journeyman carpenter, which is what I feared (because that would mean little record). He was something like what we would now call a contractor. Had his own shop, too, where he sold all manner of things (my left nut for ten minutes in that store!). Or maybe I'm reading too much into the records I

found. Actually, I suppose it's possible, considering the span of the dates, that the store was owned by a son, or even a nephew or an uncle. But it would make some sense that it was him, so I accept it. Two or three of the more solid little buildings in this village are either his work or have had more modern structures grafted onto his foundation. Isn't that a fun thought?

But for all the intense gratification of tracking him down, I've hit a dead end. Parish registers didn't come in until, what, the 1530s or so, and there just aren't that many other places to look for a fairly unknown person like this. There was no estate list or any such luxury for the guy when he died (there might have been, considering his standing), and as near as I can tell, his line died out or otherwise evaporated in the late 1700s. So here I am, frustrated. *Piscator interruptus.* Guess I better call Stan and see if I can get back on the river, though all the good hatches are over, I suppose. Maybe the Dame will take a Woolly Bugger, if I could slip it past the rules committee.

I'm calmed down now, if you were worried. It happened kind of abruptly, when I got here, even before I realized I wouldn't find what I was after. Don't know

what came over me, but I sure wouldn't want Doctor Dan taking my blood pressure any time in the past month. Whatever you do, don't tell him about this. He thinks I'm spending August at a fat farm.

Martin.

The next day!

Al,

I got it! The scent came back on, and I got it, and it's mine and mine alone!

But I get ahead of myself.

I was set to leave first thing this morning, and after I mailed your letter yesterday I did call Stan and tell him to expect me tonight. Now that I think of it, there's no reason why I can't still get there. Nothing to hold me here now that I have it.

Anyway, what happened was, after I wrote you yesterday, I decided to indulge in the consolation of a nice heavy dinner, pound down a ploughman's special at the local lard bucket. As it happened, the place was one I'd

been to a few times this week, one of the buildings Shupton might have had something to do with constructing.
It's one of those dingy little pubs the tourists would find
almost quaint if they ever got out this way, as long as they
stayed upwind. It was comforting somehow, that even
though the search had ultimately proven fruitless, at least
I had found this physical connection with the old boy. I
wanted one of his magic flies, but I had to settle for his
house-carpentry.

The barkeep is absolutely antediluvian, a turnip-
nosed chap with the diction of a goat, and the place is
filthy, but you can tell it's had its times. When I got him
talking (I gagged out a compliment about the onions), he
wound up and gave me a historical tour (why mentioning
the onions set him off on that, I don't know.) He claimed
the building was six, maybe seven hundred years old,
which sounded like at least a twenty-five-percent lie, but
practically everything inside is covered with cheap plas-
ter, phony paneling, and plastic signs, so it's hard to tell.

But I'd already been thinking about how old it was.
All week, every time I'd go in for lunch, I'd fantasize
about taking a crowbar to the whole place, as I levered
the last window sash free from its frame (even in my fan-

tasies good luck doesn't come fast), a small "jar of erthe" would roll free from its 500-year hidey-hole, drop to the floor, and shatter, revealing among its contents a single, odd-looking fly and a short note on how to tie it.

Well, eventually the barkeep said he'd meant to tell me something but kept forgetting it when I came in. His name's Shipley, by the way—close, but no cigar. Anyway, despite the impression I got from the local archives, it seems there were still Shuptons around until World War II, when two brothers by that name were killed and their wives moved off to London. Then there was only a Ship-ton woman, who kept chickens for the eggs in the 1950s. The barkeep kept talking about her for a while (as I wondered if these were the same eggs in the jar on the bar) until it dawned on me he was somehow attached to her, from forty years ago. After a while, as he droned on, I kind of tuned out everything but the rasp of his voice and looked around.

The place, as I said, was a mess, what with several centuries of cheap furnishings having been tacked onto whatever was there at first. The windows were mostly still old (a hundred years or so, I mean) glass, the hand-rolled stuff with all the waves and bubbles, and their

frames looked a lot older. The ceiling, one of those dark, high, overbeamed things, was so tarred over with human fumes that I'm sure it must have stopped taking white-wash about Cromwell's time. The bar was obviously modern, as were the stools and all the tables and chairs.

But the back end of the room was simply overwhelmed by a monolithic fireplace, bricked up with some kind of ugly efficiency stove piped into it. Its mantelpiece was a huge old log, roughly squared, still covered with the ancient axe scars and irregularities of its making, and about 20 feet long. I'd often admired it, just for its dura-bility, but now, with the droning serenade of the barkeep fading a little as he reminisced softly about the chicken woman, with the dull evening light diffused by the streaky windows, and with the ticky-tacky paneling hid-ing most of the other parts of the room where Shupton himself might actually have put hand to wood, I flashed on the man himself, or maybe myself as the man, and I saw what he would have to do if he really wanted to tell me about his fly.

He'd want to leave a trace, but he wouldn't want to tell everybody. He'd want to tell someone who was sharp enough, and discreet enough, to figure it out without

blabbing it. Someone who could admire him without wasting a world-class secret. As a practical man, a businessman, and a builder, he must have known how few things last a long time, and how long his secret might have to wait until someone came along with sense enough to recognize it.

If he decided to leave a clue on paper (and I find no evidence he could even sign his name), where would he put it? The written message is a lousy idea. People didn't own much paper in those days, or think much of caring for it. No, he would look for something more permanent. Something more durable.

Without even saying excuse me, I rose from my stool and moved slowly toward the mantel. I was looking at it differently now, not to understand its purpose but to penetrate its other possibilities. I said it was squared, but as I got closer I realized that wasn't quite true. The top was flat, and shelved out from the wall far enough to hold some old mementos—I remember a boot, for some reason. But the bottom was rounded, especially where it drove back into the wall right above the fireplace. There was only the weakest light under there, but all it showed was the usual assortment of greasy mars and dents, some

probably from drunks rising up under it after messing with the fire, some certainly from the axe that worked it into shape. No intricately carved little images, no recessed compartments. It had been a neat idea, certainly a more deserving fantasy than the jar in the wall, but no dice.

Well, rather than walk back to the bar and hold myself up on a stool, I took a seat in a big fanback chair near one end of the fireplace, and redirected my attention to the barkeep, who had never broken stride in his monologue even though I wasn't even pretending to listen there for a while. He was still telling me about his adventures with the chicken woman; you don't want to know.

About midnight, another soul had not been in all evening, and he decided to close up. By then we'd completely stopped communicating. I never did eat. I just sat there trying to generate enough gumption to light a pipe before bed. It seemed that all the weeks of squinting at old paper, all the pathetic, gutbusting food, suddenly caught up with me, and I went into some sort of metaphysical coma—no need to move, no need to think. Just sit and inhale whatever ingrown organisms drifted loose from those appallingly unclean rafters.

I might have sat there all night, for all he cared. In fact, I think he forgot I was even there and closed up

without telling me. As he walked out the back way, probably just through reflex he flipped off the light switch, leaving me sitting in the near-dark, except for a streetlight dimly shadowing the room from one window. In my condition, I didn't really mind, but it did stir me enough to decide on the pipe, at last. A few seconds and I had it lit. Then I figured that while I was on a roll and had proved I could still move, I might as well leave.

It was a matter of perfect timing, Al. Shupton couldn't have foreseen it, but if he really wanted someone to know his secret, he must have hoped for it. As I rose from my chair, I realized I was still holding the lighter, so to help me weave through the tables in the dark, I gave it a flick. At that moment, still bent partly over, my eyes happened to be on the mantelpiece, which I was seeing almost end-on and from slightly below. As the old Zippo flared up, light hit that wood from an angle the windows could never provide, and just for an instant my mind registered a faint pattern thrown into unexpected relief. I was halfway across the room before the message of my eyes registered a complaint in my brain and I stopped, realizing I'd just seen something considerably more intentional than axe marks. I turned back and resumed my position at my chair, then held the lighter up.

There in the flickering light was a curving parabola, a thin, very shallow cut (more like a gentle groove than a sharp-edged runnel) in the wood, looking for all the world like the bend of a fishing rod, arcing upside down and then slipping out of sight underneath the rounded bottom of the mantel. Moving to the fireplace and crouching so I could get a look up underneath the mantel, careful to hold the lighter so it would continue to strengthen the shadow, I saw the groove end in a very simple little design, even shallower. Light from any other angle would not have shown it, Al, not even from the fireplace itself. The man was devilishly careful. I thought of rubbing the grime off it for a better look, but I figured that might make it too noticeable, so with a combination of running my fingers along the lines and shifting the lighter all around it to catch the shadows of each part better, I could make it all out well enough.

Well, I don't dare tell you more about the design without risk of telling you too much about the fly it depicted. In truth, though, it only depicted a few key elements. I was wrong, by the way, when I said the fly probably had only one important feature; actually there are three features of the fly that raise the eyebrow, four if you

count both wings. I guess you'd have to call them wings, anyway.

Tantalized, are you?

Anyway, it was plain I had to just memorize the thing; no drawings, no rubbings on paper, no evidence but what I remember. That's what I did, then let myself out of the pub and headed to my inn. Back at my room, I dug out my kit, clamped the vise on the washstand, and got to work. His intentions were so apparent that I was pretty sure what I had to do, but I tried a few variations, just to be sure. Then all I could do was wait until light.

How much thought he must have given that, Al! Imagine how he puzzled over what to do, where to put it, and then how much time he must have spent thinking out its positioning on the mantel.

See, other than the windows and the electric ale signs behind the bar, the only light in the room comes from a single fixture in the middle of the ceiling. It has one grimy little bulb in it now—this isn't the kind of place where people want to be seen, much less be seen well— but I could see that the receptacle had just been patched onto some older wooden mount that may have hung a lantern or something, maybe one of those old candle-

holders. Shupton couldn't have anticipated electricity, but I'll bet he anticipated that the pub would always have fairly unimaginative types in charge—"That's where the light always was, so why be movin' it?" Of course that high light over the room just flattened out the contrast of the visible part of the carving—the arched rod that led you back underneath—it gave it no relief, no chance of shadow, even if someone had cut a new window and added light from another angle. Only when the light came from almost parallel with the mantel, and down low, would you see more.

What a game for him to play, so long before Zippos. I wonder who he thought would find it, or if he just enjoyed the thought of so many years of the local fishermen getting all liquored up and bragging about how good they were at it, and arguing with each other about this fly or that technique, all the while sitting within pissing distance of the Holy Grail?

But you will want to hear about the flies, won't you? Well, just before what could decently be called dawn, I was already out on the bank of this little local stream, about half a mile south of the village. I'd seen it on the way in, one of those poor misbegotten little creeks that's

endured a thousand years of cow manure and worse, but still might hide a few fish of some kind. I figured it was a good test; after all, it was probably in worse shape in Shupton's time.

Keeping my eyes peeled (you know how it is over here, I must have been fishing *someone's* water!) I tied the most likely of the flies, a #12, on a 4X tippet and rolled it across this little pool about 35 feet, up against a steeper bank on the far side (were History ever to find out about this, she would record that I was using the Orvis 7–4).

It was like a magnet, Al. Remember how the pickerels cut wakes after our bucktails at Grand Lake? Three wakes converged on the fly almost instantly. I swear one of them came fifteen feet; how the fish kept from colliding I don't know, but I was hooked to something before the fly had sunk an inch. It turned out to be a big dace, and I caught three or four more, and one crooked little brown, before reeling in and getting out of there. There was something unseemly about it all, even if it wasn't illegal.

I had to finish up this letter on the train, which arrived a couple pages ago, and I want to get it in the mail before the weekend. I think that's tomorrow. Any-

way, I'll give you a report in a couple days. Maybe send you a picture of the Dame stretched out on the grass, huh? I've got her now. What am I saying—I've got them *all* now.

M.

The Dorset Inn
Sunday, August 14

Al,

It's been a dream. I caught 64 trout Saturday, 59 today. What's the club record for a day, 23? I feel like Babe Ruth. Four of them were more than 4 pounds, even though the new riverkeeper (you won't like him—snotty as hell) claims there's nothing that big here. They came out of weeds and holes and hides that nobody here even imagines exist. This is better than electroshocking.

They didn't even care about tippet diameter. After a while I trimmed it back to 0X, which hardly fit through the eye of the hook, just so I could horse them in and get them off the hook.

It was trickier than hell handling that many fish and letting them go without being seen. (How did old Shupton keep others from seeing his fly? Were there just fewer fishermen then?) It was good luck, though it didn't seem it when I first heard, that I drew the old grainery beat. That put me farthest from the Dame (damn!), but it ensured my privacy; nobody likes fishing down there because there aren't many trout. Ha!

I've developed a system for protecting my magic, too. Friday night in my room, I suffered an attack of paranoia about someone discovering the fly. Of course it wouldn't matter much if Stan or Dot saw it when they were doing up the bed or something. They don't know one fly from another. But all sorts of other possibilities came to mind, so I shaved all the materials off the extra flies, so I would only have one. I keep it in a little plastic film canister in my fleece-patch pocket. Should I have to, I can get rid of it fast, and it's never out where people can see. Twice, guys came by, once it was even the keeper, and I saw them coming from far enough away to get the fly off the tippet and replace it with a Tups or something. It occurred to me just as I was dozing off last night that if I

were to suffer an embolism or something, I could at least try to get that one fly out of the canister and pitch it into the water where nobody would find it.

I'm still on such a high, I can't imagine going back to town for that dreary book project, but I can't just stay here, either, catching these stupid fish by the barrel. Tomorrow I'll check with Stan about when I can get the Dame's water again. Meantime, maybe I'll do some honest fishing with my other flies, but that doesn't sound very appealing to me.

Marty
P. S. I wonder how big I'd have to tie it for Islamorada?

Saturday, August 20

Al,

This is the first I've been able to write. The gout or some damn thing grabbed me during the night after I wrote, and then I got these vicious gutaches, and I puked for two days. It was hellishly embarrassing, because I couldn't even make it to the pot, and Stan and Dot (and once I think even Megan, God forbid) had to clean me

up. I was so miserable I barely remember anything before about Thursday, when I was able to listen to the doctor they'd called in from down the road. He gave me this raft about my bad habits, sounded just like Doctor Dan except that he didn't seem to mind the tobacco as much.

So I guess the holiday is over. Stan is checking on my flights, so maybe we can have lunch soon. I figure a couple more days lounging around here won't hurt first, and maybe one more try at the water. Maybe I'll get the Dame after all.

Marty

Tuesday, August 23

Al,

I guess I was sicker than I thought. I'm still weak as a kitten, just kind of plod over to the WC every now and then, and once a day wobble down to the reading room to pick out a few books to sleep with. I'll write again when I can.

M.

Saturday, August 27

Al,

Still here, but doing much better, thank you. They've taken such wonderful care of me, I hate to leave. Actually I feel better than I have for years. Had to cut down on the swinishness at table, put the pipe away. I bet I've shed 25 pounds, though the first half of it was ejected rather abruptly.

A most uncharacteristic thing happened this morning—Megan actually volunteered a word to me. She'd brought me breakfast, for which I was thanking her excessively when she said (in wild violation of the normal restraint of these people, and looking me straight in the face!), "We're pleased you enjoy it, Mr. Martin—we've never been sure you liked our food."

Perhaps all that close contact when I was semiconscious made her feel free to speak. Of course I was mortally ashamed of myself; I'm afraid she may have heard me some time when I was ranting about how awful British food is. But now that I think of it, I guess I haven't been making much sense, considering my appetites. I never

gave it much thought until she said something. I suppose I enjoyed kicking such an easy target—everyone makes fun of British food, you know. But it must have seemed quite odd to them, what with the way I inhale everything they cook over here. The difference between Taste and taste, I suppose.

Anyway, I do have other things to tell you. This morning I put on a dressing gown and with firm step paraded my new health right down to the reading room. I'd been revisiting the best writers more each day, but today I was able to really dig in, and my what a wonder it's been.

Skues knew. I'm just sure of it. He found his way to the Fancy, and, true sport that he was, he kept it to himself and stayed with the game despite having an easy way out. He could have let all that quest for imitation go, he could have been even more immortal than he is, simply by writing one short note to *The Field* with a drawing of the Fancy. What a man.

But let me tell you how I worked this out. Think back to the last time someone revealed a secret to you, something they'd been keeping from you for a long time. If you're like me, you immediately picture things that

happened—conversations, actions, whatever—that now, in retrospect, you realize were clues. You suddenly see that the secret holder was telegraphing something to you, either consciously or subconsciously avoiding something. Maybe he suddenly was just a tad too forceful in changing the subject of a conversation, or in some other way walked you down a different road than the accustomed one. The change didn't even register consciously on you, or earn a place in your active memory, but it involuntarily comes to mind at all once, and you smile, and say, "Oh, so that's what was up!"

Well, I've been through something like that, and more than once. In fact, I suspect that others must have known, too. First, here's how I worked it out with Skues. You know he's my favorite. All those little notes and essays are perfect toilet reading, and the man was just so damn comfortable to read, an old slipper. Well, I got to reading him during my waking times about five days ago, and of course there's seven or eight books, now that most all of his notes and letters have been gathered up, which is a lot of conversation. (It would be impossible to figure this out from very many of the older writers because they didn't leave enough volume of output for it to show up.)

At first, just grazing here and there in his books, I sensed nothing different. But after a while, the hints were there. The first two or three I hardly registered. As I was reading, the Fancy would come to mind unexpectedly, but I would just read on, thinking it was just my own obsession randomly surfacing in my thoughts now and then. But finally I had to see it; he'd get to talking about some fly-tying trick, and I'd recognize its possible connection to the Fancy, and then, just a little too abruptly, he'd veer away and continue in a slightly safer vein.

So that set me to looking for others. I don't know that I found any for sure. I have to wonder if Skues found the Fancy on his own or if someone told him (did he track down Shupton from some completely different direction?).

What's interesting is that I think it's easier to tell if someone *didn't* know. I can tell you for sure that Halford didn't, and as little as we have from Ronalds, I'd bet a month of your pay that he didn't either. The only earlier American who might have known was Gordon; there are a couple hints in his wonderful notes and letters. But of course he and Skues were pen pals, so it's impossible to guess who told who. I think if I spent the time with *The Fishing Gazette* and *Forest and Stream* or maybe *The*

American Angler, I could get a handle on which other writers from back then were in on it. I wish McBride had written more—there was a first-rate mind in a second-rate business.

Gordon and Skues were so open-minded about fly materials and structure, and put so many years into it, that either or both of them could have just tripped over it one day, though actually seeing the elements of it is only the beginning. You'd have to come to the final product a step at a time, combining several unappealing elements, and that means you have to overcome a whole pile of prejudices we've inherited about proportion and realism and "style."

We're not really that smart, you know. Well, we may be smart but we're not especially original. We copy, we modify, but we rarely create, being such slaves to tradition, fashion, and our own predispositions.

But back to the reading room. After I'd realized that most of the older writers didn't leave me enough words to justify a search for clues, I got into that shelf of the really old periodicals (I think I'm the only one to open them since the club inherited them), the ones behind the glass. There's an article I thought I remembered reading about, in the *Sporting Magazine* (out of London, I guess) from

1828, with an illustration of some supposed French flies of the time. I'd never looked it up before, but I remember the article—I read somewhere, probably in *The American Fly Fisher,* that it was all supposed to be a hoax, because the flies were so funny looking and were said by the writer to be for carp. But rereading it (what modern English-language outdoor magazine would publish a whole article in French?) I don't know. They aren't the Fancy, but I could tell that the guy had a hint, whoever he really was. If you were to look that article up yourself, next time you're here, you'd see what I mean about us being unoriginal. There's something there you will never have seen in any other flies since. It would only take you about 30 percent of the way to the Fancy, so I don't mind telling you this.

What it makes me wonder about, though, is how many guys actually tied the Fancy and didn't know what they had. Think how many of us there have been, all those amateurs—how many? millions, I suppose—grinding out monstrous little patterns for everything from trout to bass to bluefish. Even as surprising as the Fancy is, it could happen that someone just made it by accident.

Say you sat down and felt experimental, so you just tied up all kinds of wild things. We all do that at some point. Some of them we never use. Imagine the star-crossed sap who did that, and then jammed the weird-looking thing into a corner of the box and never used it. Or, even worse, used it one day and broke it off on the first fish, and just figured it was a lucky cast, or, even worse, couldn't remember what it looked like well enough to tie another one!

Skues seems to have been the last. I made a quick run through the most prolific moderns, and though there's one or two Brits who might have had a chance to know, none of the Americans do. All those bug-fondlers and techno-empiricists, so busy trying to turn a religion into a science—Swisher and Richards, Borger, LaFontaine, Schwiebert—don't have a clue, though the more I think about some of his recent stuff, the more I think that if LaFontaine could relax a little bit he might have a chance at it.

Think of all those intense overachieving young fly fishermen you see out there in their handsome outfits, all

of them out to conquer this theoretical world, and they don't even understand what's really waiting at the end of the rainbow.

That's probably just as well. Now that fly fishing has become such an industry (a fortune runs through it . . .), I'd hate for some greedy bastard to get hold of this, patent it, and ruin everything. Imagine the stink. All the state fish and game people would be passing regulations outlawing it, but poachers could clean out a creek in hours. And the lotus-eaters would be cranking out essays and editorials on what's become of our sport.

They shouldn't discover it for another reason, Al. Very few of us have the strength of will that Skues must have had, to disallow himself the use of such a gift. I sure as hell don't have that kind of control; I want to gimp out there right now and show the Dame who's boss. Skues was right to keep fishing—to just put the Fancy aside and get on with the struggle—but nobody should even know about this. I mean, it's not just that it makes fishing too easy; if that was the only problem, you *could* just outlaw it, like dynamite. The problem is, it makes the struggle irrelevant.

The damned, ironic thing about fly fishing and fly tying is that the whole goal is to discover something just like the Fancy, but if you do the game's over. It's not a sport any more. You win, but you lose. If you bring the Grail home to Camelot, you're going to be celebrated and canonized, and have a great time that night, but what are you going to do with yourself the next morning? Nobody should have this thing.

All at once I'm pooped out, so to speak, and I have to get back to my room. More later.

Marty

The Dorset Inn
September 23, 1994

Mr. Albert Boehringer
24385 Post Mills Road
Grosse Pointe Farms,
Michigan

Dear Mr. Boerhinger,

Please forgive my not answering your letter more promptly, but we're still trying to restore a little order here. We were pleased to hear that the services went so well. Seeing Mr. Martin stretched out so horribly there along the river, it was impossible to think of him coming to a peaceful rest on the other side of the world only four days later. He seemed to be doing so well, the doctor was sure there was no harm in him taking a little time on the river.

No need to thank us for caring for the remains and all. Everybody from the embassy and the airport was very kind, and the few other guests we had were quite understanding about the break in our attentions.

We were very fond of Mr. Martin. I suppose we should be grateful the stroke was so powerful; the coroner thought he could only have suffered a moment before he was gone.

But let me address your questions. First, it's true that he had what must have been the fish you call the Dame on the bank. In fact, she was still on his line, and I supposed at the time that the exertion or excitement is what brought on the attack. We are having her done, of course, with a nice plate. I think the reading room would be a nice place; he so enjoyed it there.

I must say, I always thought it amusing, your stories of this fish you had named. None of the other regulars ever seemed to see it. But when I saw the look on the face of Lance, the new keeper, when we brought it in, I understood a little better what it meant to you. He tells me a 10-lb., 4-oz. fish is simply impossible in this water, that a pike would hardly even get that big. I'm not sure he believes even yet it really came from the Dorset.

The fly is another matter. You know I don't fish, Mr. Boehringer, but I am obliged to know enough to keep an eye out for the unusual. You Americans have such different ideas about what is proper, but had I seen the fly he was using under less tragic circumstances I should have

had to report it to the membership committee. It was one of those enormous hairy things, I think you call them Wooly Boogers? Of course I promptly disposed of it; no use in saying anything now. I'll say he was using a Tups, when we do the plate.

I believe that takes care of it. Again, please accept our most heartfelt sympathies for the loss of your friend.

Sincerely,
Stanley Frampton
Prop.

P. S. Rereading your letter I discovered that I had overlooked one of your questions. You are right that Mr. Martin's vest was somehow left behind; I just found it hanging in the equipment room. At your suggestion I checked the fleece pocket, and indeed there was a film canister in it. But it wasn't empty, as you supposed. There was one fly in it. I assumed you might want it or you wouldn't have asked, so I am attaching it to the bottom of this letter.

Acknowledgments

I'm especially grateful to the people who read the manuscript and made all manner of helpful comments: Sally Atwater, David Detweiler, Richard Hoffmann, Nick Lyons, Dianne Russell, Judith Schnell, and John Varley. They may notice that I did not always take their advice, but I usually did, and they all affected my understanding of the story I was trying to tell here. The staff of *British Heritage* magazine helped with advice on food and food attitudes.

I'm also grateful to Richard Hoffmann, Professor of History at York University, Ontario, for his enormous scholarly contribution to our understanding of angling before 1500. It was his review of William Braekman's book on the *Treatyse*, which I published in *The American Fly Fisher* in 1982 when I was editor of that wonderful

journal, that started me thinking about using Anthony Shupton in a work of fiction (I must therefore also express my gratitude to Mr. Braekman for his book). Since then, Richard has provided the fishing community with a steady flow of new publications and treatments that have enriched our appreciation of the nature of medieval fly fishing beyond anything we could have imagined.

I'm a historian of sorts too, so there is a lot of actual history mixed in with the fiction in this book; I didn't just cook up a bunch of names to provide authentic-sounding atmosphere. Most of the historical details in this book, including the various historical fishing authors mentioned, the basic information about William Worcester, and the modern fishing historians and writers (all treated rather disrespectfully by the protagonist), are real. Even the 1828 French-language article about the carp flies is real. Fishing history is so full of quirky characters and neglected episodes that it requires very little fictionalizing.

My agent Richard Balkin provided his usual fine guidance, and David Detweiler and Judith Schnell at Stackpole Books showed faith in a fairly unusual idea for

a book. Since first sharing the idea for this story with David (himself an author of notable fiction involving fly fishing), during lunch in Harrisburg some seven or eight years ago, we've both kept busy with other books, but he's never failed to encourage me to get around to writing this one.

Finally, David Ledlie, my successor as editor of *The American Fly Fisher*, has been my chief advisor in matters of fishing history for nearly twenty years now, and I take this opportunity to thank him on the dedication page.

Paul Schullery
Yellowstone, 1996